# A Benjamin Blog
## and his Inquisitive Dog
# Guide

# Canada

Anita Ganeri

heinemann
raintree

Edited by Helen Cox Cannons and Tony Wacholtz
Designed by Steve Mead
Original illustrations © Capstone Global Library
Limited 2015
Illustrated by Sernur ISIK
Picture research by Svetlana Zhurkin
Production by Helen McCreath
Originated by Capstone Global Library Limited
Printed and bound in China by CTPS

18 17 16 15 14
10 9 8 7 6 5 4 3 2 1

**Library of Congress Cataloging-in-Publication
Data**
Ganeri, Anita, 1961-
  Canada / Anita Ganeri.
     pages cm.—(Country guides, with Benjamin
Blog and his inquisitive dog)
Includes bibliographical references and index.
ISBN 978-1-4109-6847-0 (hb)—ISBN 978-1-4109-
6855-5 (pb)—ISBN 978-1-4109-6870-8 (ebook)  1.
Canada—Juvenile literature. I. Title.
  F1008.2.G36 2015
  971—dc23                          2014013394

**Acknowledgments**
We would like to thank the following for permission
to reproduce photographs: Alamy: Alan Douglas,
18, John Zada, 20; Dreamstime: Peter Van Der
Heyden, 23; Getty Images: Farah Nosh, 14, Robert
McGouey, 24, Yvette Cardozo, 17; iStockphotos:
RyersonClark, 10; Newscom: Danita Delimont
Photography/Peter Langer, 7, Getty Images/AFP/
Geoff Robins, 19, Icon SMI/Minas Panagiotakis, 22,
WENN/ZOB/CB2, 12, ZUMA Press/Carlos Osorio,
16; Shutterstock: FER737NG, 15, FloridaStock, 11,
Ildi Papp, 21, Ivan_Sabo, 25, karamysh, cover, 13,
kavram, 4, Paul Stringer, 28, pavels, 8, Protasov
AN, 27, SF photo, 26, Songquan Deng, 12 (inset),
29; SuperStock: Science Faction/Ed Darack,
9; Wikipedia: D. Gordon E. Robertson, 6; XNR
Productions, 5.

Every effort has been made to contact copyright
holders of material reproduced in this book. Any
omissions will be rectified in subsequent printings if
notice is given to the publisher.

All the Internet addresses (URLs) given in this
book were valid at the time of going to press.
However, due to the dynamic nature of the
Internet, some addresses may have changed,
or sites may have changed or ceased to exist
since publication. While the author and publisher
regret any inconvenience this may cause readers,
no responsibility for any such changes can be
accepted by either the author or the publisher.

007200CTPSS15

Some words are shown in bold, **like this**. You can find
out what they mean by looking in the glossary.

# Contents

Welcome to Canada! . . . . . . . . . . . . . . . .4

Vikings and Inuits . . . . . . . . . . . . . . . .6

Lakes, Mountains, and Islands . . . . . . .8

City Sights . . . . . . . . . . . . . . . . . . . . .12

People of Canada . . . . . . . . . . . . . . .14

Feeling Hungry . . . . . . . . . . . . . . . . . .20

Ice Hockey and Stampedes . . . . . . . .22

From Timber to Apple Trees . . . . . . . . .24

And Finally... . . . . . . . . . . . . . . . . . .26

Canada Fact File. . . . . . . . . . . . . . . .28

Canada Quiz. . . . . . . . . . . . . . . . . . .29

Glossary . . . . . . . . . . . . . . . . . . . . . .30

Find Out More . . . . . . . . . . . . . . . . . .31

Index . . . . . . . . . . . . . . . . . . . . . . .32

# Welcome to Canada!

Hello! My name is Benjamin Blog, and this is Barko Polo, my **inquisitive** dog. (He's named after the ancient explorer **Marco Polo**.) We have just returned from our latest adventure— exploring Canada. We put this book together from some of the blog posts we wrote along the way.

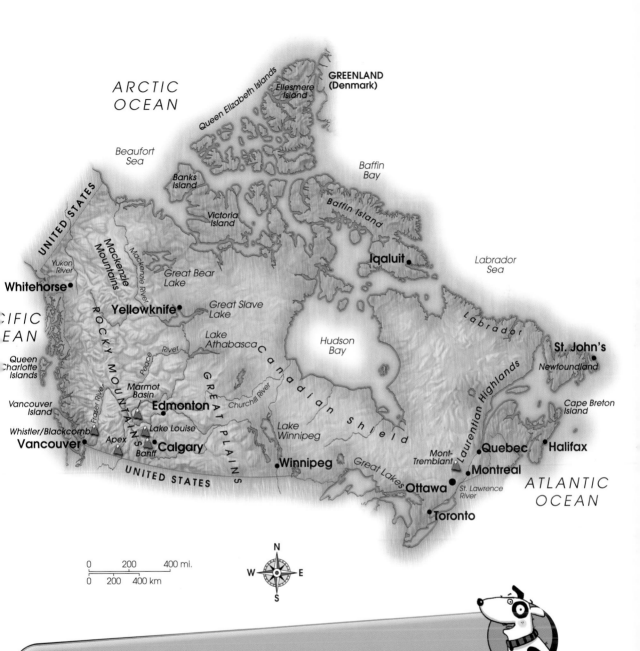

ARCTIC OCEAN

GREENLAND (Denmark)

Queen Elizabeth Islands

Ellesmere Island

Beaufort Sea

Banks Island

Baffin Bay

Victoria Island

Baffin Island

UNITED STATES

Yukon River

Whitehorse

Mackenzie Mountains

Mackenzie River

Great Bear Lake

Iqaluit

Labrador Sea

PACIFIC OCEAN

Yellowknife

Great Slave Lake

ROCKY MOUNTAINS

Lake Athabasca

Peace River

Canadian Shield

Hudson Bay

Labrador

St. John's

Newfoundland

Queen Charlotte Islands

GREAT PLAINS

Marmot Basin

Edmonton

Churchill River

Lake Winnipeg

Laurentian Highlands

Cape Breton Island

Vancouver Island

Fraser River

Lake Louise

Apex

Banff

Calgary

Whistler/Blackcomb

Vancouver

Winnipeg

Great Lakes

Mont-Tremblant

Quebec

Halifax

UNITED STATES

Ottawa

St. Lawrence River

Montreal

ATLANTIC OCEAN

Toronto

0    200    400 mi.
0   200   400 km

N
W    E
S

# BARKO'S BLOG-TASTIC CANADA FACTS

Canada is an enormous country in North America. It has the longest coastline in the world, with the Pacific, Atlantic, and Arctic Oceans on three different sides. On land, Canada is joined to the United States in the south.

# Vikings and Inuits

Posted by: Ben Blog | March 17 at 3:15 p.m.

It is our first day in Canada and I've come to L'Anse aux Meadows, on the northern tip of Newfoundland. This is where the **Viking** Leif Ericsson landed in around 1000 CE. He was the first European to reach North America. I'm off to explore this Viking town.

## BARKO'S BLOG-TASTIC CANADA FACTS

This is Iqaluit, the capital of Nunavut (a huge area in the far north of Canada). In 1999, the land was officially given to the **Inuit** people, who had lived there for thousands of years. The name *Nunavut* means "our land" in the Inuit language.

# Lakes, Mountains, and Islands

Posted by: Ben Blog | April 4 at 9:31 a.m.

From Newfoundland, we headed to Lake Superior. At 31,700 square miles (82,100 square kilometers), it's the world's biggest freshwater lake. You can see how it got its name! It's one of the five Great Lakes on the border with the United States. The others are Michigan, Huron, Erie, and Ontario.

## BARKO'S BLOG-TASTIC CANADA FACTS

Mount Logan stands 19,551 feet (5,959 meters) tall and is the highest mountain in Canada. To climb it, you have to fly to one of the **glaciers** at the base of the mountain. Then it's a 19-mile (30-kilometer) hike to the top.

Our next stop was Baffin Island, back in Nunavut. Huge parts of northern Canada lie in the Arctic Circle and are covered in ice and snow for most of the year. Luckily, the **Inuit** are experts at surviving. They wear pairs of mukluks (sealskin boots) to keep their feet warm.

## BARKO'S BLOG-TASTIC CANADA FACTS

Normally, polar bears in Hudson Bay hunt for seals on the sea ice. But if there isn't much food, they sometimes wander into the town of Churchill and **scavenge** in people's garbage cans.

# City Sights

Posted by: Ben Blog | May 6 at 2:11 p.m.

Today, we arrived in Toronto, the biggest city in Canada, and went to the CN Tower. At 1,815 feet (553 meters) high, it's one of the tallest towers in the world. You can walk around the outside of the tower, on a ledge near the top. Very scary!

# BARKO'S BLOG-TASTIC CANADA FACTS

Stanley Park is in the city of Vancouver. Visitors can walk, run, or cycle along the Seawall, a path overlooking the Pacific Ocean. Then, if you are feeling tired, you can ride the miniature railroad.

# People of Canada

The **Inuit** and First Nations people have lived in Canada for thousands of years. These people are Haida, a group of First Nations people from British Columbia in the northwest. Many Canadians today are **descended from** settlers who came from Great Britain and France.

14

Canada has two official languages: English and French. French is mostly spoken in Québec. The First Nations and Inuit people also have their own languages. This street sign is in English and French.

Children in Canada start school at the age of five or six and stay until they are 16 or 18. Afterward, some continue their studies at a college. Most subjects are taught in English, but in Québec, there are also many French-language schools.

16

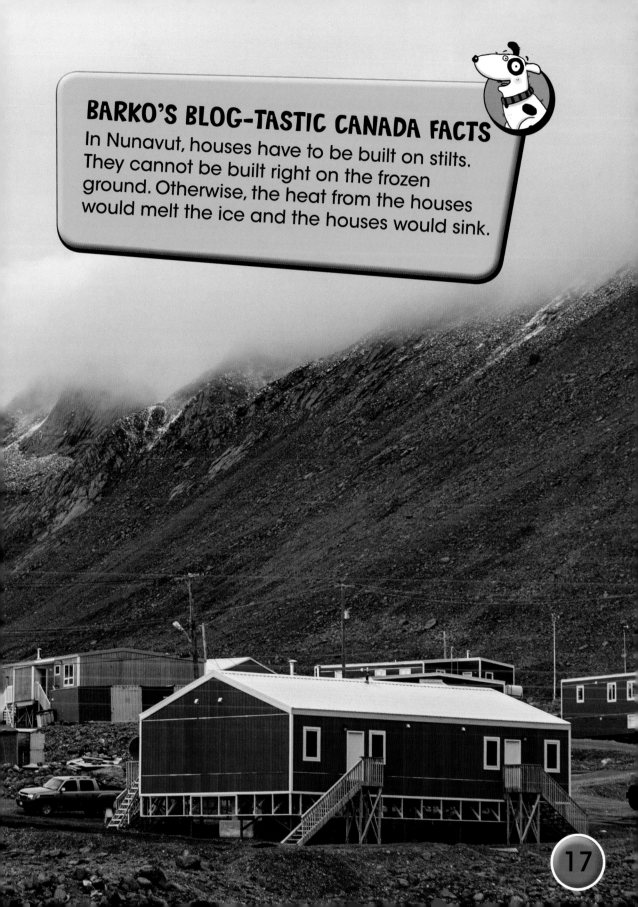

**BARKO'S BLOG-TASTIC CANADA FACTS**
In Nunavut, houses have to be built on stilts. They cannot be built right on the frozen ground. Otherwise, the heat from the houses would melt the ice and the houses would sink.

We're here on Vancouver Island, with the Kwakwaka'wakw people. Traditionally, they catch salmon for food. Every year, they hold a special ceremony to say thank you to the salmon. There's a Salmon Dance and a feast—with lots of salmon to eat, of course.

On July 1, Canadians celebrate Canada Day to mark the day in 1867 when Canada became a country. On Parliament Hill in Ottawa, there's a thrilling display by the Snowbirds flight team.

# Feeling Hungry

Posted by: Ben Blog | August 28 at 5 p.m.

After another full day of sightseeing, we stopped for a quick bite to eat. There was plenty to choose from on the menu, but I decided to give poutine a try. It's made of French fries topped with cheese curds and gravy. You can eat it with chicken, bacon, or even lobster.

# BARKO'S BLOG-TASTIC CANADA FACTS

Canada is famous for maple syrup, which is made from the **sap** of maple trees. I like it on pancakes best, but people also like to mix it into oatmeal.

# Ice Hockey and Stampedes

Posted by: Ben Blog | November 12 at 1:10 p.m.

Stopping off in Montreal, we got tickets for an ice hockey game. Ice hockey is fast and furious, and it's the most popular winter sport in Canada, with an ice rink in every town. We're here to watch the Montreal Canadiens, one of the top teams in the country.

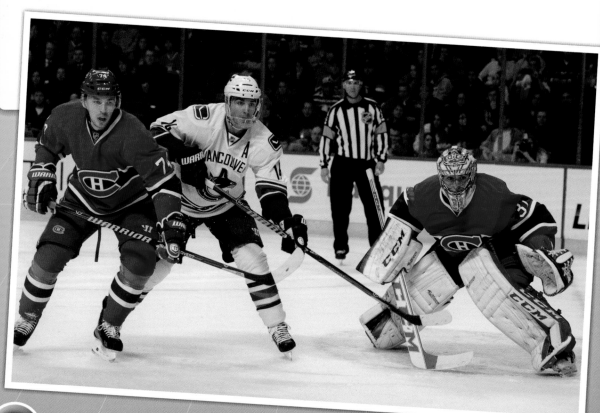

## BLOG-TASTIC CANADA FACTS

Every year, in July, more than a million people flock to the city of Calgary for the famous Calgary Stampede. At the top of the program is the **rodeo**, with events such as riding a bucking bronco and bull wrestling. Yikes!

23

# From Timber to Apple Trees

Posted by: Ben Blog   |   January 3 at 10:53 a.m.

Back in British Columbia, we visited this giant sawmill. It is where logs are cut into smaller pieces of wood. More than half of Canada is covered in forests, and wood is very important. The wood and wood products, such as paper, are sold all over the world.

# BARKO'S BLOG-TASTIC CANADA FACTS

Want to try a crunchy apple? Farmers in Canada grow apples in large **orchards** along the shores of Lakes Ontario, Erie, and Huron. They also grow grapes, blueberries, peaches, plums, cranberries, and pears.

# And Finally...

Our last stop was Niagara Falls, three whopping waterfalls on the border between Canada and the United States. This is Horseshoe Falls on the Canadian side. Here, the water falls around 173 feet (53 meters). You can watch it land from a tunnel near the bottom. What a splash!

## BARKO'S BLOG-TASTIC CANADA FACTS

This is Banff National Park in the Rocky Mountains. It's a stunning place, with ice-capped mountains, **glaciers**, lakes, and forests. It's also home to some amazing animals, including **caribou**, wolves, and grizzly bears, such as this one.

# Canada Fact File

Area: 3,855,103 square miles
(9,984,670 square kilometers)

Population: 35,427,524 (2014)

Capital city: Ottawa

Other main cities: Toronto, Montreal, Vancouver

Languages: English, French

Main religion: Christianity

Highest mountain: Mount Logan
    (19,551 feet/5,959 meters)

Longest river: Mackenzie River
    (1,025 miles/1,650 kilometers)

Currency: Canadian dollar

# Canada Quiz

Find out how much you know about Canada with our quick quiz.

1. Which country is Canada joined to?
a) Greenland
b) United States
c) Russia

2. Which is the world's biggest lake?
a) Lake Erie
b) Lake Huron
c) Lake Superior

3. What is maple syrup made from?
a) maple tree **sap**
b) maple tree leaves
c) maple tree bark

4. Where is ice hockey played?
a) on a field
b) on a track
c) on a rink

5. What is this?

**Answers**
1. b
2. c
3. a
4. c
5. the CN Tower

29

# Glossary

**caribou** large North American reindeer

**descended from** related to people from a long time ago

**glacier** river of ice that flows from a mountain or sheet of ice

**inquisitive** interested in learning about the world

**Inuit** people who have lived in the Arctic for thousands of years

**Marco Polo** explorer who lived from about 1254 to 1324. He traveled from Italy to China.

**orchard** place where fruit trees are grown

**rodeo** display of horse-riding skills and rounding up cattle

**sap** thick, sticky substance under the bark of a tree

**scavenge** search for something among garbage

**Viking** people who lived in Scandinavia about 1,000 years ago

# Find Out More

## Books

Greenwood, Barbara. *The Kids Book of Canada*. Toronto: Kids Can Press, 2007.

Hurley, Michael. *Canada* (Countries Around the World). Chicago: Heinemann Library, 2012.

## Web sites

Facthound offers a safe, fun way to find Internet sites related to this book. All of the sites on Facthound have been researched by our staff.

Here's all you do:

Visit *www.facthound.com*

Type in this code: 9781410968470

# Index

Arctic  10

Baffin Island  10
Banff National Park  27
bears  11, 27

Calgary Stampede  23
Canada Day  19
cities  12–13, 19, 28
CN Tower  12
coastline  5

First Nations  14, 15, 18
food  18, 20–21
fruit growing  25

Great Lakes  8

ice hockey  22
Inuit  7, 10, 14, 15

Lake Superior  8
languages  15, 16
L'Anse aux Meadows  6

maple syrup  21
Montreal  22
Mount Logan  9, 28

Niagara Falls  26
Nunavut  7, 10, 17

people  7, 10, 14–15, 28
poutine  20

religion  28
rodeos  23

schools  16

timber industry  24
Toronto  12

Vancouver  13
Vancouver Island  18
Vikings  6

wildlife  11, 18, 27